GREETINGS FROM
PARIS

Joel Porter

THUNDER BAY
P·R·E·S·S

San Diego, California

Establishment of a City

From fishing to fashion

Today, Paris is famously known as "the City of Light," but when a Celtic tribe, called the Parisii, settled on the Île de la Cité around 250 BC, it was little more than a small fishing village. Being located on the river Seine, the settlement became a prosperous trading post for the Parisii, but its strategic position also attracted unwanted attention. Despite a valiant revolt, the Celts were powerless to prevent the invasion of Julius Caesar's Roman army in 52 BC. Under Roman rule, the city, known then as Lutétia, expanded onto the left bank of the Seine, with the construction of grand public buildings such as a forum, baths, and an arena.

By the early fifth century, however, the Romans' power had effectively collapsed, and over the next few centuries, Paris was controlled by a succession of dynasties. "France" itself was established, and Paris was made its capital, with the accession of Hugh Capet to the throne in 987 AD.

During the Middle Ages, Paris flourished as an important center of political power,

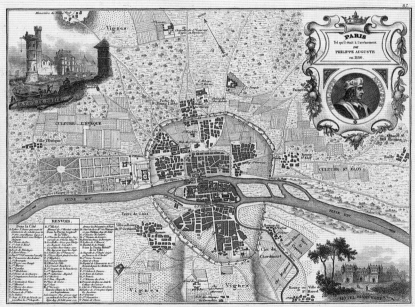

Above: A map of Paris as it would have looked in 1180. The city has spread to the right and left banks of the Seine by this time, but is still much smaller than modern Paris.

religion, and learning, with the establishment of universities, such as the Sorbonne in 1253,

Above: Louis XIV chose the sun as his personal emblem because of its associations with Apollo, god of peace and the arts.

and grand cathedrals like Notre Dame, completed in 1345. It was also a time of great upheaval, however, with outbreaks of plague, war, and revolution.

Louis XIV, known as the Sun King, developed Paris in grand fashion during the seventeenth century ("the great century"), with buildings such as the Hôtel des Invalides, originally a home for wounded veterans, with its magnificent Dôme Church. Much of the population, however, still lived in squalor and poverty among the city's crowded, narrow medieval streets.

It was only after two popular revolutions against the monarchy that much of Paris, as we recognize it today, was created. Under the rule of Napoleon III in the mid-nineteenth

century, Paris was transformed into the most magnificent city in Europe.

Baron Haussmann was appointed prefect of the Seine in 1853, and under his direction the city was completely modernized. The crowded, unsanitary streets were demolished and replaced with broad avenues and boulevards; large public parks such as the Bois de Boulogne were opened, and sewer systems were laid beneath the city streets.

From a Celtic fishing settlement to a sophisticated modern Paris, "The City of Light" had begun to take shape.

Left: Haussman extensively redesigned the Place de l'Étoile, the meeting point of 12 avenues, seen below.

French Revolution

Birth of the Republic

On July 14, 1789, a crowd of revolutionaries stormed the Bastille prison in Paris, sparking one of the most important events in French history. Before the attack, opposition toward King Louis XVI had been growing for some time, as a result of mass inflation, poverty, and famine. In an attempt to appease the nation, Louis agreed to discuss the establishment of a national constitution. Mistrust of the king endured, however, fueled by rumors that he had sent troops to surround Paris.

Animosity toward the crown soon reached breaking point and Paris was consumed by chaos, culminating in the attack on the Bastille, which was viewed as a symbol of royal repression. Its governor, Marquis de Launay, refused to surrender at first, and a violent battle ensued before the prison finally fell. The revolutionaries came away with only seven rescued prisoners and de Launay's decapitated head on a pike as their prize, but their victory struck a huge blow against the foundations of Louis's power.

Things worsened for the king and the royal court in October, when thousands of women marched on Versailles, protesting ever-increasing bread prices. An unimpressed Marie-Antoinette famously dismissed them, saying

Left: Portrait of King Louis XVI. Louis is the only King of France ever to be executed.

Below: This gilded figure, the "Génie de la Liberté," stands atop the July Column, a symbol of civilization and freedom.

"let them eat cake," but after a violent standoff at the palace, the King had little choice but to return to Paris.

In 1791 a national constitution was finally established, which left Louis XVI as little more than a symbolic figurehead. For the openly republican Jacobins, however, this was not enough, and they continued to argue for the complete abolition of the monarchy. Continuing disagreements saw the rule of this constitutional monarchy collapse during the following year, culminating in an attack on the Tuileries on August 10, 1792. The royal family was captured and became prisoners of the radical Paris Commune, led by the zealous revolutionary Robespierre. On September 22, the monarchy was officially abolished and the date was proclaimed "Day one of year one of the French Republic."

The unsettled period that followed became known as "the terror," as anyone suspected of opposition to the new republic met a gruesome end at the guillotine. Louis XVI was executed on January 21, 1793, and Marie-Antoinette on October 16. Robespierre's bloody reign could not endure, however, and he was arrested and executed in July 1794. Moderate republicans now sought to gain control, and a new government, the directory, was established in 1795.

Greetings from
• *Paris* •

Wartime Paris

The years of darkness

From about 1890, Paris blossomed—the first motorcars took to the streets, the Lumière brothers invented cinema, the first Metro line was built, and the city was decorated by Art Nouveau. The outbreak of World War I in August 1914, however, brought the glitz and glamour of Paris's *belle époque* (beautiful era) to a dramatic halt.

The German army advanced quickly on Paris, and the Allied forces found themselves in steady retreat. By September 2, the Germans were just fifteen miles from the capital, prompting the French government to take refuge in Bordeaux. The city was spared invasion, however, by the First Battle of the Marne, in which 6,000 troops were sent to the front line in Paris taxis to aid the Allied counter-attack. By September 13 the Germans were in full retreat. Paris was safe, but France had suffered a huge loss of life by the time the war ended in 1918.

Paris suffered a far worse fate in World War II, during the four-year Nazi occupation. The city fell to the Germans on June 14, 1940, without much resistance, and became the western headquarters of the Nazi command.

The swastika soon adorned many public buildings, including the Eiffel Tower. Hitler himself came to Paris on June 23, 1940, visiting the Eiffel Tower, the Opéra, and Napoleon's tomb.

The Jewish population of Paris suffered greatly during the occupation. Thousands were rounded up and deported to concentration camps in Germany, from which most never returned. Many attempted to fight this persecution, however, either by hiding Jewish families, or obtaining false papers from sympathetic government officials.

After the Allied invasion of Normandy in June 1944, German troops were forced to retreat east, and their power started to collapse. On August 23, Hitler ordered his commander, General von Choltitz, to destroy Paris. He took no action, thereby leaving the majority of Paris's architecture unscathed. Liberation finally arrived on August 25 when the Allied forces, led by the French General Leclerc, entered Paris. That afternoon, outside the Hôtel de Ville, Charles de Gaulle delivered a rousing speech to a euphoric crowd, in which he praised the French people and their capital city. Victory parades on the Champs-Elysées took place the following day—Paris was a free city once more.

Left: French women joyfully greet American soldiers as the Allied forces liberate Paris.

Far left: French resistance fighters deal with Nazi snipers.

Right: Under the Arc de Triomphe lies the Tomb of the Unknown Soldier. The remains of this unidentified WWI soldier were interred here in 1920, in tribute to all those nameless men who died during the war.

The Eiffel Tower

Symbol of Paris

The sight of the Eiffel Tower rising dramatically above the city is the ultimate symbol of Paris. Designed by the engineer Gustave Eiffel, it was built as part of the celebrations for the 1889 Exposition Universelle, to commemorate the centenary of the French Revolution. Although it is now one of the most famous monuments in the world, many Parisians viewed it with disgust at the time of its completion, with one writer, Leon Bloy, deriding it as "a truly tragic street lamp."

A remarkable feat of industrial engineering, the tower took 300 workers just two years, two months, and five days to complete. Proclaiming Paris a new city for a new era, its graceful ironwork lattice was a daring and unorthodox design, and despite the initial detractors, the tower soon won its admirers. At 984 feet, it was the tallest building in the world, a record it held for forty-one years until New York's Chrysler building was completed in 1930.

The tower was due to be dismantled after twenty years but was allowed to remain standing by the French government as

Above: Photograph of Gustave Eiffel in 1889. Eiffel also constructed the ironwork frame for the Statue of Liberty.

it proved useful for experiments in radio communications. A permanent antenna, added to the tower in 1957, is still used today to broadcast both radio and television stations. The antenna also increased the total height of the tower to 1,063 feet, making it still the tallest building in Paris.

Above: An Eiffel Tower paperweight

The thought of Paris without the Eiffel Tower is unimaginable today—the strength and beauty of its design epitomize the French capital. Attracting almost 7 million visitors a year, it is one of the most popular paid-for attractions in the world, and is an essential part of one's Paris experience, even if just glimpsed from afar. The tower is not just to be looked at, however, as it also offers magnificent panoramic views of the city for those who journey to its third tier observation deck.

Top right: Paris 1889 Exposition

Below right: Men painting the tower in 1924. It is repainted every seven years, requiring sixty tons of paint!

Far right: Every July 14, the Eiffel Tower is lit up by a spectacular fireworks display, part of the Bastille Day celebrations to commemorate the storming of the Bastille.

Below: Sequence of images showing the stages of construction. Remarkably, the first and fourth images were taken just one year apart, highlighting how quickly the Eiffel Tower was built.

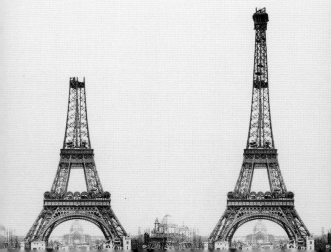

Notre Dame Cathedral

Gothic splendor

At the very heart of Paris, on the Île de la Cité, stands the magnificent cathedral of Notre Dame. Completed in 1345, no other building is more closely associated with

Above: Notre Dame Cathedral illuminated at night—one of the most romantic sights in Paris.

Left: A Notre Dame gargoyle surveys the city of Paris, protecting the cathedral from harmful spirits.

the history and development of Paris. The French capital had long been a Christian city, ever since St. Denis arrived in the third century to evangelize its people, but with the completion of Notre Dame it was established as one of the holiest cities in Europe.

Construction of the cathedral had begun after the Bishop Maurice de Sully decided that Paris needed a new cathedral of suitable grandeur. He first ordered the demolition of St. Stephen's cathedral, which stood roughly where Notre Dame stands today, and also of several houses in the surrounding area. Work finally got underway, tradition has it, when Pope Alexander III laid the foundation stone in 1163.

1050

1050

900

750

600

450

300

150

feet

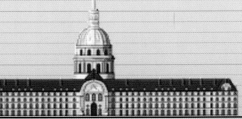

Obélisque de Luxor   La Cathédrale Notre-Dame de Paris   Dome Des Invalides   Le Panthéon   Arc de Triomphe

The construction of Notre Dame came at a time when the gothic style of architecture was gaining prominence. The cathedral is widely considered to be one of the finest examples of French gothic architecture, demonstrated by magnificent features such as the 42-foot rose windows, the ogival arches that form the vaulted ceiling, and the external flying buttresses. The original design did not include the flying buttresses, but as the walls of the nave grew higher, they became a necessary addition in order to support the huge structure. Notre Dame was one of the first buildings in the world to employ this architectural technique, and it eventually became a standard feature of the gothic style.

Right: Detail from the *Portal of the Last Judgment,* the central doorway on the west side of the cathedral.

Below: The spectacular South Rose Window is made up of eighty-four stained-glass panes, divided into four circles.

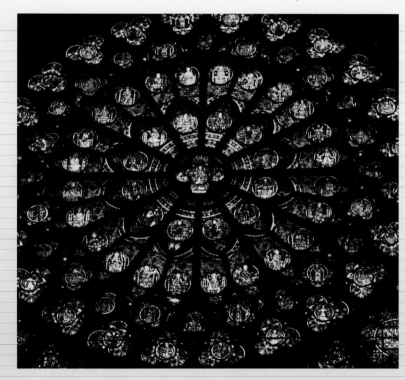

Notre Dame suffered its darkest hour during the French Revolution when much of the cathedral was desecrated. Religion was banned by the revolutionaries; the cathedral was rededicated to the Cult of Reason and much of its religious imagery was destroyed. It was even used during this period as a wine warehouse. Fortunately for Notre Dame, Napoleon restored religion in 1804 and used the cathedral for his coronation ceremony. The building had suffered much damage, however, and in 1845 a restoration program was undertaken by Eugène Viollet-le-Duc, which included the construction of a new spire. Notre Dame was restored to its former glory.

Colonne de Juillet   Bibliothèque Sainte-Geneviève   Opéra Garnier   Eiffel Tower   Tour Erard

Montmartre

A bohemia of art

The steep *butte* (hill) of Montmartre, rising 425 feet above the city, is a unique corner of Paris. Its long, tree-lined staircases, winding alleys, and hidden squares lend the area a romantic village charm, which has long attracted people searching for an alternative lifestyle.

This was never truer than in Montmartre's heyday, from the mid-nineteenth century into the early twentieth. At this time, the area played host to a lively community of bohemians—artists, writers, and poets—who inhabited the quarter and drew inspiration from their surroundings. The district was famous for its bars, cabarets, and exotic nightclubs, and the bohemian artists were no strangers to these establishments. Pop into Au Lapin Agille in the early twentieth century and you may well find Picasso drinking absinthe at the bar; enter the Moulin Rouge, and there is

Henri Toulouse-Lautrec sketching the wild scene before him; spend an afternoon dancing and drinking at Le Moulin de la Galette and perhaps you will be captured in Renoir's famous painting. Elsewhere, you might see Camille Pissarro, Vincent van Gogh, Henri Matisse, or Edgar Degas, along with countless other artists.

To the rest of Paris's citizens, Montmartre was a hotbed of depravity, but to these artists it was a place of free expression, of boundless energy and excitement, which provided the ideal setting for their own experiments with style and form in their work.

Montmartre's most prominent landmark is

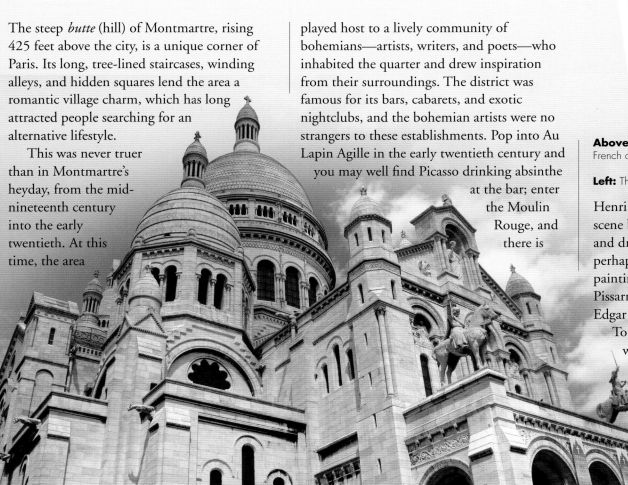

the monumental Basilica of the Sacré-Coeur. This huge white church, constructed in the Romano-Byzantine style between 1875 and 1914, is dedicated to the Sacred Heart of Christ. Perched on the hill, at the highest point in Paris, you can catch a glimpse of its unmistakable white dome from all over the city. After climbing the steps to the Sacré-Coeur you can experience breathtaking views of Paris spread out below.

Right: The famous red windmill of the Moulin Rouge cabaret, established in 1889

Below: Steep stairways lead up to Montmartre's summit.

Below right: Artists at work in the Place du Tertre

Cemeteries

A mini-Paris for the dead

In Paris, even the cemeteries are places of beauty and romance. At Père-Lachaise cemetery in the northeast of the city, tombs are arranged along winding cobbled lanes and rolling tree-lined hills, making it a sought-after burial place. The picturesque setting also makes it a popular tourist destination, and Père-

Below: Jim Morrison's grave, complete with tributes.

Lachaise is said to be the world's most visited cemetery.

Aside from its eerie beauty, Père-Lachaise owes its popularity to the many famous citizens among the 300,000 people who are buried here. Great Parisians who have helped to shape the city's history, such as Victor Hugo, Colette, Balzac, Marcel Proust, Delacroix, Edith Piaf, Baron Haussmann, and Gertrude Stein are all laid to rest here. One of the most visited graves belongs to Oscar Wilde, who died in Paris in 1900. His headstone, a naked male angel carved by Sir Jacob Epstein, originally had genitalia, but legend has it that the head keeper of the cemetery was so offended by it that he castrated the figure. His grave has also become notorious for the graffiti and lipstick marks left on the headstone by visitors as a sign of their admiration for the writer.

Another much-visited grave belongs to Jim Morrison, the lead singer of The Doors, who passed away in a Paris hotel room in 1971.

His tomb attracts a constant stream of fans, some of whom leave graffiti and tributes similar to those on Wilde's grave.

Opened in 1804, Père-Lachaise was named after Louis XIV's confessor, Père de la Chaise. Originally it was considered too far from the center of the city, only becoming popular when the remains of Molière and La Fontaine, along with the supposed remains of medieval lovers Abelard and Héloïse, were transferred here. It was not long before the numbers of people buried here began to increase and with each famous resident, the fame of Père-Lachaise itself grew.

Montparnasse cemetery, which opened just twenty years later, in 1824, boasts a similarly impressive list of famous names, including Jean-Paul Sartre, Simone de Beauvoir, Charles Baudelaire, Samuel Beckett, and Serge Gainsbourg.

Left: (top to bottom) Sir Jacob Epstein with his sculpture for Oscar Wilde's memorial; the grave of Victor Noir which famously became a fertility symbol; and the grave of Proust.

Below: Père-Lachaise cemetery is hauntingly beautiful.

The Louvre

The world's most visited art museum

The history of the Louvre museum dates back to 1190, when King Philippe-Auguste built a robust fortress at the city's western end in order to improve its defenses. But as Paris expanded in the mid-fourteenth century, new ramparts were built farther out, and the role of the Louvre fortress as a defensive structure became redundant. Charles V (1338–80) first converted the fortress for use as a royal residence, but it was under the rule of François I (1494–1547) that much of the Renaissance-style palace we see today was constructed. It was also François who invited Leonardo da Vinci to Paris and purchased the *Mona Lisa*, which is now the star piece of the museum.

Successive kings left their marks over the centuries, expanding and improving upon the Louvre's buildings. Royal interest in the palace had already declined after the construction of Versailles, however, and during the revolution it was converted to a museum. It opened to the public on August 10, 1793, the first anniversary of the monarchy's demise.

In 1981 the Grand Louvre project was launched, which sought to modernize and reorganize the whole museum. As part of this project, the famous glass pyramid entrance was designed by the Chinese-American architect I.M. Pei and opened in 1989.

Above: The *Mona Lisa* hangs alone on a wall in the Louvre's Salle des Etats, behind unbreakable glass.

Below: The magnificent Apollo Gallery at the Louvre features works by artists such as Girardon, Le Brun, and Delacroix, under its huge 50-foot-high ceiling.

Over its long history, the Louvre has become one of the largest and most famous museums in the world, with 35,000 works of art on display, ranging from antiquities, to European paintings, to *objets d'art*. It is the most-visited of all art museums, attracting millions of visitors each year who come to marvel at its unrivaled collection and the grand buildings of the Renaissance palace.

Immediately adjacent to the grounds of the Louvre are the Tuileries Gardens, the largest public gardens in Paris. They were once the royal gardens of the Tuileries palace, originally built by Henry II's widow, Catherine de Medici. Louis XIV had the gardens completely redesigned, however, and in 1667 they were opened to the public for the first time. Much like the Louvre, the gardens have been subject to frequent redesign and modernization over time, but they have remained a popular destination.

Right: Crowds admire the Venus de Milo, a famous Ancient Greek sculpture depicting the goddess Aphrodite.

Below: The lush grounds of the Tuileries Gardens open out from the main courtyard of the Louvre. They are the perfect place to relax after a visit to the museum.

The Art of Paris

A city consumed by art

A stroll through the hilly streets of Montmartre takes you to the former workplace of many great artists, but to see some of their most magnificent paintings, you must visit the Musée d'Orsay. Opened in 1986, the museum fills the space of the former Gare d'Orsay, an impressive Beaux-Arts railway station opened at the 1900 Exposition Universelle. Trains stopped serving the station in 1939, and in 1977 the decision was taken to convert the building to a museum, while retaining much of its beautiful original architecture.

Covering the hugely influential period of 1848–1914, the museum houses a superb collection of Impressionist and Post-Impressionist artworks. Paris-based artists such as Claude Monet, Pierre-Auguste Renoir, Camille Pissarro, and Edgar Degas were at the forefront of the Impressionist movement during the 1870s and '80s. Coinciding with

Above: The Musée d'Orsay retains the original iron and glass roof of the former railway station.

the modern development of the city, these artists celebrated the new Paris in much of their work. Monet, rather fittingly, loved to paint stations and made several paintings of the Gare Saint Lazare, one of which hangs in the Musée d'Orsay today. The changing light, clouds of steam, and movement of the trains, made this an ideal subject for the Impressionist painter.

Paris was the art capital of the world, with the Impressionists leading the way. Post-Impressionists such as Paul Cezanne, Paul Gauguin, and Vincent Van Gogh developed their own radical styles and kept Paris pre-eminent as the twentieth century beckoned. Paris was a city consumed by art. The Art Nouveau movement, most famously documented in Hector Guimard's metro station entrances, dressed the city in elegant, flowing shapes. Even public toilets built in the early twentieth century were decorated in the beautiful Art Nouveau style, a fine example of which can still be seen by the church of La Madeleine.

In 1903 the first Paris Autumn Salon was launched in order to exhibit the work of innovative young artists who would not necessarily be recognized by the conservative official salon. The show became a significant force in the development and status of modern art and helped establish the reputations of many artists such as Henri Matisse. The American writer Gertrude Stein and her brother Leo were huge patrons of the modern art world, and their collection at 27 rue de Fleurus had a worldwide reputation. Their gallery also hosted important social gatherings—it was here that one of the Steins' favorite artists, Pablo Picasso, first met Matisse.

Above: Picasso's 1906 portrait of Gertrude Stein. When someone commented that Stein didn't look like her portrait, Picasso replied, "She will."

Above left: Detail from *At the Moulin Rouge* by Henri Toulouse-Lautrec (1892). This painting is one of the artist's most famous works.

Literary Paris

A magnet for great writers

Above: Early twentieth-century shoppers browse the bookstalls alongside the Seine. The market still thrives today.

The literary history of Paris has a richness that few other capital cities could claim to match. Many of the nation's greatest writers have lived in Paris, finding inspiration here for their most celebrated works. The French novelist Victor Hugo lived much of his life in Paris, in a house on Place des Vosges, where he wrote his masterpiece, *Les Misérables*. In one chapter, entitled "Here Is Paris, Here Is Man," his adoration of Paris is clear, when he praises "this prodigious city" as an all-encompassing "total . . . the ceiling of the human race."

Many other great writers, including Charles Baudelaire, Emile Zola, Marcel Proust, Colette, and Honoré de Balzac, spent much, if not all, of their lives in Paris. Baudelaire penned his most famous volume of poetry, *Les Fleurs du Mal*, while living on rue d'Amsterdam; Balzac lived all over Paris, writing from midnight until 5:00 a.m. fueled by endless cups of black coffee; and in 1906, Proust retired into his second floor apartment on Boulevard Haussmann, to begin the seven-volume *Remembrance of Things Past*.

It was not only the French literary masters who felt the magnetic pull of Paris. Attracted by a vibrant art culture, a moral and social

Above: George Whitman's bookstore is still a focal point for writers, hosting regular poetry readings and literary events.

liberty, and cheap living, many of the great English-language writers of the twentieth century have flocked to the French capital. Ernest Hemingway, the quintessential American in Paris, said of the city: "to have come on all this new world of writing . . .

was like having a great treasure given to you." Hemingway spent several years in Paris during the 1920s; here he wrote *The Sun Also Rises*, and developed his direct narrative style under the mentorship of Gertrude Stein, American writer and poet.

Through Stein, Hemingway was introduced to many expatriate writers, including Ezra Pound, F. Scott Fitzgerald, and James Joyce, who often gathered at the famous Shakespeare and Company bookshop (left). The shop was of particular significance to Joyce, as its owner, Sylvia Beach, was the first to publish his novel, *Ulysses*, in 1922. In the late 1950s, the shop, now moved to 37 rue de la Bûcherie and owned by George Whitman, served a similar social function for American Beat writers such as Allen Ginsberg, William Burroughs, and Gregory Corso.

Right, clockwise from top left: The great French writer Marcel Proust; Colette, renowned novelist and performer; Allen Ginsberg, American Beat Generation writer; Les Deux Magots—a favorite café of writers such as Jean-Paul Sartre and Ernest Hemingway.

Cuisine

Gourmet capital of the world

For Parisians and visitors alike, food is never far from the mind. With thousands of cafés, bistros, restaurants, and food markets, the city rightly deserves its reputation as one of the greatest food capitals in the world.

An afternoon sipping coffee in one of the city's celebrated cafés is an essential Paris experience. For centuries, Parisians have come to cafés to meet friends, relax, or simply read the paper over a cup of coffee and a croissant. The first café in the world was Le Procope in St. Germain, which opened in 1686 and still exists today. One of its most famous patrons, the philosopher Voltaire (1694–1778), would supposedly come here to work every day, fueled by forty cups of his favorite coffee and chocolate mixture!

When it comes to finding a more substantial meal, there is no shortage of options: a simple, hearty meal in a cozy neighborhood bistro; an extravagant classic such as *fruits de mer* at an upmarket brasserie; or exceptional haute cuisine at one of the city's

Above: *Fruits de mer*—a classic seafood feast.

many fine-dining restaurants. Boasting ten restaurants with three Michelin stars, and chefs such as the innovative Pierre Gagnaire and the legendary Joël Robuchon, Paris offers you some of the finest food in the world.

Dining out is by no means confined to French cuisine either—thousands of immigrants from all over the world have made their home in Paris, bringing with them their national cuisines, from North Africa, the Caribbean, and Vietnam—to name three of the most popular.

Parisians also love to cook, of course, and there is no better place to buy produce than at one of the city's many open-air food markets. Since the Middle Ages, these markets have been an integral part of city life, providing freshly picked fruit and vegetables, organic meat, fresh fish, farmhouse cheeses, an array of breads, pastries, and much more. The market experience is always exciting too, with stallholders calling out the latest bargains and enticing customers with free tasters.

Right, clockwise from top left: Opened in 1896 and still going strong, Chartier serves classic brasserie-style food; a tempting display of the freshest fungi on a Parisian market stall; La Coupole is one of the most famous brasseries in Paris. Today, tourists flock to see its Art Deco murals, but it was once the haunt of artists such as Picasso and Man Ray; À la Mère de Famille has barely changed since the day it opened in 1761. Located in Montmartre on the rue du Faubourg, it sells the most delicious sweets and chocolate.

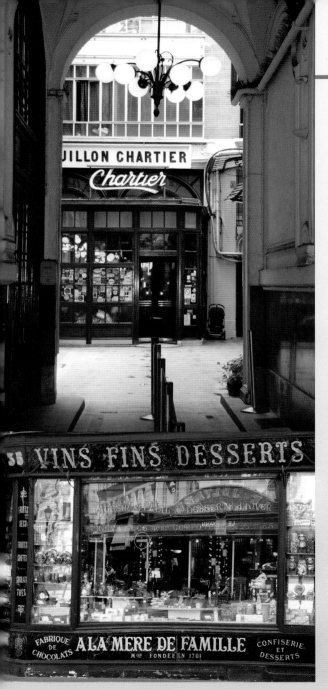

Haute Couture

Paris—the home of high fashion

For many people, Paris means one thing: fashion. Since the reign of Louis XIV (1643–1715), the rest of the world has looked to Paris for inspiration on what to wear. Jean-Baptiste Colbert, Louis XIV's Finance Minister, recognized the commercial importance of fashion for the French economy, sending salesmen across Europe with dolls dressed in costumes made by Paris dressmakers to promote their work. In the eighteenth century, portraits of Queen Marie

Above: rue du Faubourg Saint-Honoré is perhaps the premier shopping street in all of Paris.

Antoinette wearing the latest luxurious styles spread the fame of Paris fashion, and dressmakers in other countries eagerly copied the styles.

In the nineteenth century, an Englishman named Charles Worth came to dominate the world of high fashion in Paris. Now known as the father of *haute couture*, Worth began to show his designs on live models, and rich Americans as well as European aristocrats flocked to the city to buy his clothes. The term *haute couture,* a guarantee of high-quality design and materials, is protected by French law.

One of the most influential fashion names of the twentieth century was Coco Chanel, who opened her first shop in Paris in 1913. Her simple, classic designs, such as the "little black dress," were a huge success, and in 1919 she opened her couture house in rue Cambon, where it remains today. In 1947 Christian Dior, another legendary

Left: A model presents a creation by Jean Paul Gaultier.

Far left: Pioneering French designer Coco Chanel

Paris couturier, launched his famous "New Look," featuring extravagant fabrics and very full skirts. After the shortages and hardships of the war years, Dior's clothes shocked the fashion world and were an instant success.

Other designers, notably Yves St. Laurent, Christian Lacroix, and Jean-Paul Gaultier, keep Paris at the cutting edge of fashion in the twenty-first century. Twice a year, these designers, among many others, show off their new collections at Paris Fashion Week, the most hotly anticipated event in the industry calendar.

Being a fashion capital has also made Paris an internationally renowned shopping destination, and many haute couture stores—such as Dior, Fendi, and Louis Vuitton—populate the city's two main fashion shopping streets, Avenue Montaigne and rue du Faubourg Saint-Honoré. Aside from the big-name fashion houses, the historic Marais district also boasts many boutique fashion and jewelry stores. Other famous shopping destinations in Paris are the *grands magasins,* department stores such as Galeries Lafayette, Au Printemps, and Bon Marché. Here you can indulge not only in high fashion, but also gourmet food in their food halls and restaurants.

Right: The interior of Galeries Lafayette department store and a selection of chic and exclusive handbags.

Sport in Paris

Soccer, tennis, and the Tour de France

The sporting life of Paris is perhaps not the best-known aspect of the city, but it is certainly not to be overlooked. Soccer is undoubtedly the nation's favorite sport, and the capital's team, Paris Saint-Germain, is one of the most successful in the country. Having played in the top Ligue 1 since 1974, they have won two league titles, eight French cups, and three league cups. The team's home is the Parc des Princes stadium, a venue renowned for its white-hot atmosphere, especially when arch rivals Olympique de Marseille are visiting for "Le Classique," the most anticipated match in the domestic soccer calendar.

The Parc des Princes was also used as the national soccer stadium until the Stade de France was completed for the 1998 Soccer World Cup, which France hosted. It was at this new stadium, on July 12, that France recorded their greatest achievement, beating Brazil 3-0 in the final to be crowned world champions. That night, Paris erupted as more than a million ecstatic fans crammed the Champs-Elysées to celebrate their victory.

The Stade de France still hosts all French soccer internationals and domestic cup competitions; in 2000 and 2006, it was the venue for the UEFA Champions League Final. The stadium is also frequently used for domestic and international rugby matches, and hosted much of the Rugby World Cup in 2007.

A major tournament held every year in

Below: Cyclists on the final stage of the Tour de France.

Paris is the French Open tennis championship. As the second of only four grand slam tournaments in the tennis calendar, and the only one to be played on clay, it is one of the most prestigious events in the sport. It is played over two weeks between late May and early June, at the Stade Roland Garros, where it has been held since 1928.

It is the Tour de France, cycling's premier event, that provides Paris with its greatest sporting moment. Although the route of the race changes each year, the final enthralling stage is always in Paris, bringing the riders down the Champs-Elysées and past some of the city's greatest landmarks, including the Louvre, the Tuileries, and the Arc de Triomphe.

Right: Matches in play at the French Open tournament.

Below: The French soccer team celebrate their 1998 World Cup Final victory over Brazil, played at the magnificent Stade de France, (below right).

The Modern City

A new age for Paris

The second half of the twentieth century saw the completion of a number of buildings that brought Paris into a new age of modernization. The Pompidou Center, opened in 1977, marked the beginning of this development with its high-tech, revolutionary design. By placing functional structures, such as its steel skeleton, escalators, and water ducts, on the outside of the building, the architects Richard Rogers and Renzo Piano were able to create a flexible and uncluttered indoor space for museum and exhibition areas. And perhaps more importantly, they made a shockingly new and unforgettable exterior.

Following the success of the Pompidou Center, Paris's urban landscape was continually developed in the 1980s and '90s, with a civic building program known as the *Grands Projets*. Initiated by François Mitterrand, French

president from 1981 to 1995, the program aimed to provide Paris with several modern monuments that would revitalize the city. The Louvre pyramid and the Musée d'Orsay

were both part of the *Projets*, despite the latter having actually been started before Mitterrand took office.

One of the finest of the *Grands Projets* is the

Above: The Opéra Bastille was designed by Carlos Ott. It is the home of the renowned Paris Opera, the city's leading opera company.

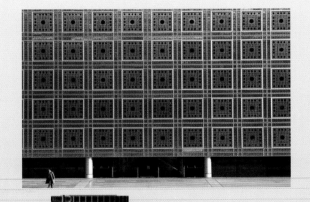

Left: The beautiful south wall of the Arab World Institute. The building houses a museum, library, auditorium, restaurant, and offices.

Tour Fugue	Tour de Flandre	Cheminee du front de seine	Tour Montparnasse	Hotel Meridien Montparnasse	Hotel Concorde Lafayette	Tour Rive Gauche

750

600

450

300

150

feet

Arab World Institute, which was designed by Jean Nouvel and opened in 1987. Combining modern materials, such as metal and glass, with traditional Arab architecture, the building is a successful link between the Islamic world and the West. Its south wall is made up of 1,600 high-tech metal screens, each containing twenty-one irises that control the amount of light let into the building. Their design is based on *moucharabiyahs*, carved wooden screens found on the outside of buildings throughout the Arab world.

Other *Projets* included the Ministry of Finance, the National Library of France, and the Opéra Bastille, which opened on July 14, 1989, to mark the 200th anniversary of the fall of the Bastille. Another of the *Projets* opened that month was the Grande Arche, situated amongst the skyscrapers of La Défense business district. The Grande Arche, made of glass and concrete, is like a twentieth century Arc de Triomphe, a celebration of modernity rather than military glory.

Left: The colorful exterior of the Pompidou Center

Below: The Grande Arche, nestled among the skyscrapers of La Défense business district

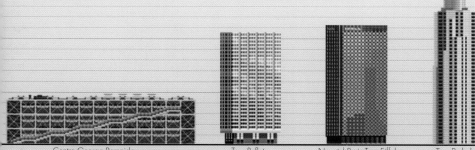

Centre George Pompidou   Tour Reflets   Novotel Paris Tour Eiffel   Tour Prelude   La Geode   Louvre Pyramid   Tour Cristal   Tour de Lettres

Wish You Were Here

The most romantic city in the world

Paris is the world's number one tourist destination, visited by millions of people every year. Beautiful, sophisticated, and full of world-famous landmarks, it never fails to enchant. And so many of its streets and buildings are familiar, from movies and paintings, that even on your first visit, you feel at home in this glorious city.

What will be the highlights of your trip— the memories that will stay with you? Perhaps a lazy morning sipping coffee in a sidewalk café; your first breathtaking glimpse of Notre Dame; shopping in the grand stores on the Champs-Elysées; or an afternoon admiring some of the most spectacular art in the world in the Pompidou Center?

Or perhaps your favorite moments might be of the famous romantic atmosphere of Paris—a never-to-be-forgotten sunset stroll along the banks of the River Seine or a candlelit dinner in a cozy bistro? One thing is for sure: Paris will weave its magic spell over you and draw you back time and time again.

Above: A postcard celebrating Ferdinand Ferber's flight over the Champs-Elysées

Top right: A ferris wheel built for the 1900 Exposition Universelle, a world's fair held in Paris

Center right: L'avenue de l'Opéra. This Haussman-designed avenue runs from the Louvre to the Palais Garnier, seen here in the background.

Right: The Place de la Bastille, circa 1918

Left: Humorous postcard by Éditions Gani, Paris

Je crois qu'il a repéré son étoile
Seems to me he's found his star!

The Louvre Museum, Paris
© Corbis

POST CARD

PLACE
STAMP
HERE

_____

_____

_____

_____

Paris at night under the gaze of a Notre Dame gargoyle
© Corbis

POST CARD

PLACE
STAMP
HERE

_____

_____

_____

_____

Paris at dusk
© Corbis

POST CARD

PLACE
STAMP
HERE

_____

_____

_____

_____

Metro sign in the Latin Quarter, Paris
© Corbis

POST CARD

PLACE
STAMP
HERE

_____

_____

_____

_____